At the Edge of Everything

ISBN: 978-1-945335-33-4 | eBook ISBN: 978-1-945335-34-1
LCCN: 2024944917
10 9 8 7 6 5 4 3 2 1

Common Notions   Common Notions
c/o Interference Archive   c/o Making Worlds Bookstore
314 7th St   210 S. 45th St.
Brooklyn, NY 11215   Philadelphia, PA 19104

www.commonnotions.org
info@commonnotions.org

Discounted bulk quantities of our books are available for organizing, educational, or fundraising purposes. Please contact Common Notions at the address above for more information.

Cover design by Josh MacPhee
Layout design and typesetting by Joe Caffentzis / Suba Murugan
Printed on acid-free paper

At the Edge of Everything
Collected Poems

George Caffentzis

COMMON
NOTIONS

Brooklyn, NY
Philadelphia, PA
commonnotions.org

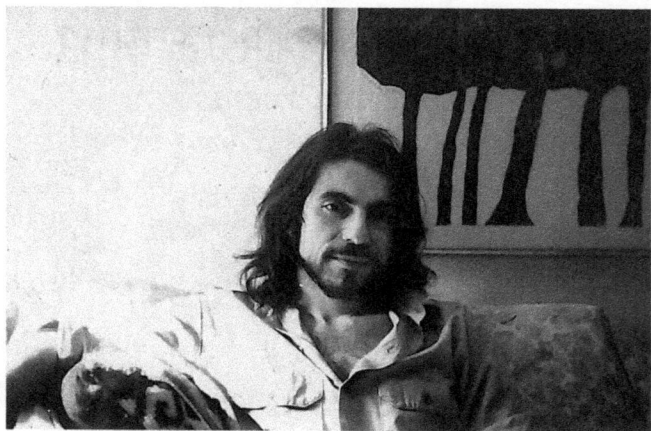

Preface

Those who are familiar with George Caffentzis'
work, from his trilogy on the Philosophy of Money
to the many articles that he has published in *In
Letters of Blood and Fire* and *No Blood For Oil!*, will
not be surprised by this book of poems. Even when
writing in prose, Caffentzis is creative and poetic.
His language—rhythmic, provocative, full of bitter
humor—is that of a man who from an early age
(thirteen, in fact) was reading the poets of the
Beat generation. The selections in this book come
from a broad collection of letters scribbled in
notebooks over many years, showing an impellent
need to find other forms of expression and other
moments of ruptures of the daily routines.

Caffentzis' poetry is generated from the
experience of the different worlds that have
shaped his life: the world of the Greek community
of which he was part, of his childhood trips to
Greece, of his father and uncles' Cube Steak
diner in Brooklyn, of the radical groups he later
joined, and later his years teaching in Nigeria.
Throughout them runs the desire for a different
world and staunch refusal to compromise with the
injustices of the past and the present.

Silvia Federici, September 2024

Introduction

I have never considered myself a poet, yet, from my adolescence, poetry has been a constant company in my life. Only recently, however, I have begun to collect poems that I had scattered through notebooks, backpages of articles and other occasional spaces. The desire to see them as one work is partly stimulated by the recognition of recurring themes, at times in syntony with those inspiring my political writings. Among them are the memories and the nostalgia for the Greek world of my childhood, my grandmother's house facing the Taygetus Mountains, the pleasures and troubles of love and political organizing, and with the passing of years, the mourning of dead friends and comrades, and above all the never-ending pleasure of playing with words.

This book collects some of the poems that have accompanied this journey. Ordering them has certainly been a valuable exercise, part of the archival work to which I am more and more inclined as I am drawn to rethinking the different trajectories of my life. But it has not been an easy task. The division of the book in three parts only appears to be a chronological one. But it actually corresponds to particular phases of my development and encounter with the world.

I decided to begin the book with my poems from the '70s because this was a time of crisis and major change in my life as well as in the broader political arena. The '70s saw the end of my marriage, cause of a tremendous bitterness that percolates in some of the poems. They also saw the beginning of an intense political engagement, centering on my participation in the creation of *Zerowork*, a political journal inspired in its content by the theories of the Italian New Left, feminism, and the politics of the Wages for Housework campaign. The end of that project in 1978 is symbolic in my memory of both the end of the revolutionary season inaugurated by the civil rights movement, the Freedom Rides, and the antiwar movement and, on the other end, the beginning (with the oil embargo and the financial war waged against New York) of neoliberal globalization and Reaganism. Of these momentous historical developments only some traces are present in the book: the conversation with a friend turned "urban pioneer," the experience of unemployment and exile from New York for the sake of a job, the penetration of the economic crisis into every personal, even sexual relation. Similarly, the poems collected under the headline "Tales of Empires" capture only moments of the powerful change which took place in my life, starting in 1983, when to escape the sense of political asphyxiation that characterized the early '80s in the US, I went to teach at the university of Calabar, a town at the border between Nigeria and Cameroon.

Arriving in the country at the time when a debate was raging as to whether or not the government should accept an IMF deal, imposing severe austerity measures, I was drawn very soon into the political organizing of students and teachers against the plan. The poems, however, express those moments when memories visited me, the distance from home providing a filter through which to assess the meaning of past relations and events. Prominent among them are memories of my father and mother and the Greece that I encountered in my maternal uncle's home, near Sparti, where I traveled with my mother at an early age. This was a Greece of magic—the magic of the Taygetus Mountains, the orange groves and the dragon flies. But as the years passed, I became aware of the political situation and the ravages produced by the fascistization of the country in the aftermath of the civil war of the '40s. This was a reality that touched me personally as I learned that a relative had participated in the assassination campaign of peasant leaders that Britain and the US sponsored to destroy the partisan movement that had fought against the Nazi/fascist occupation of the country. "Pilgrimage to a transvestite saint" is inspired by that realization.

The encounter with death—personal and political—the death inflicted by the barbarous regimes the US has not only supported but instigated in Latin America, the death of beloved friends and comrades, the death announced by my own failing powers, is the theme of my last poems in the new millennium. But the spirit in which they have been written has not been lamentation but rather resistance, celebration of friendship, and of the lives of those who stood in the way of the colonial/capitalist devastation of the earth. As for my own personal journey through 'this Earth of man/womankind' I found it intriguing to return at the opening of the book to my first poem that was published in the journal of the Brooklyn Technical High School where I studied, in 1962. I found it among my writings that I had saved from the ravenous jaws of my paper trash bin. I read it with some surprise because it contained a critique of (capitalist) technology that was beginning to take shape in the late 1950s in the face of the possibility of nuclear warfare and has since been an element of all my political work (there were "duck and cover" exercises beginning in grade school). I remember my early skepticism towards the urgent tone of the civil defense personnel which I now understand as part of a campaign to terrorize us and gain our acquiescence towards the constantly growing military budget and lethal bombs' arsenal. As my poems show, that skeptical youth, aware of the destructive power harboring behind the glitter of the world in which we live, and still thirsting for the sight of the cliffs, the forests, the skies and the seas, has never died in me.

New York, 2024

Futile Phantasy [1]

Softly sliding down slopes of air,
Ragged ridges of rough granite below
With wide, thin wings of wood iron-brown.

In supreme speed scarring the clouds,
He gazes from the gleaming glass and sees
Forms flowing into a flat mass.
A falcon-flight above forests and sea,
The man imagines a mastery over objects below
(Colors of cliffs creating new domains.)

Imperial and immense in imagination, shattering clouds,
Into torn tangled tensions of broken purity,
Dividing the density of diffuse atoms into a vacuum.

A futile phantasy, forgotten controls,
And the dizzy death dive downwards,
Smashing into a still spring meadow.

Sea, cliff, forest and sky.

[1961]

---

[1] This is my first poem, published in 1961 in *Horizons*, A Literary-Art Publication of the Brooklyn Technical High School.

To the Cube Steak [2]

To the Cube Steak
place of many encounters
drunken sailors looking for a fight
my father and I in the cellar
mixing whiskey with water
and packing the bribe for the precinct
ensuring the cops would come
when the sailors pulled the knives.
Uncle Spiro in the corner
cursing the priests and the politicians
"No politics in this place"
screams my mother.
"Here we can only have
Food and drinks."

To George, from Silvia
[January 2024]

---

[2] The Cube Steak was the diner that George's father ran with
his three brothers on 9th Street and 5th Avenue in Park Slope,
Brooklyn, from the late 1930s to the mid-1970s. It was a 24-hour
diner that served primarily sailors and dockworkers at a time
when New York was still one of the main ports in the US. The
whole family worked in it. George has spoken so often about it
that I felt I could write this poem myself by simply rehearsing
his words.

1970s
Love / Politics / Greece

A Spider in my shoe

A spider in my shoe
Mama, oranges and rabbits
Giagia, my grandmother,
In the goat house
Eating darkness
On her trousseau
Knitting, knitting, knitting.

[1969]

Equivalences

We searched the
          equivalences
through the night,
          you saw by my fingers I
was a stickler for
                    fair trade
                    and I
          felt you weigh the tightness of
                              your edge.

Want to fuck your
                    garlic hair:
                    exchanged at:
          two nights of laddered
          deception.

Want to suck your floating
                    balls:
          going at:
          five days at the corner.

Want to tongue
the far side of your cunt:
          which is worth
                    precisely:
one tub of blood.

Want to see your face flattened
with dawn sleep:
                    just:

two toes
severed in torment.

> You wondered at the count
> while I registered it.

[1975]

Who can sleep at night any more

Who can sleep at night any more
with the crisis coming on
and only backs in bed?

So at four in the morning
you rise up
to get your cigarettes
and return with a curious ball
I noticed on the ledge
in the afternoon
and had forgotten
though its paleness
had stuck in me somewhere.

It lay seamless, hermetic
in your palm before me, full of pearl light
—do you know what this is?—
as you turn it
a tiny hook latch appears
you stop and ask me to lift it open
it looks too small
but with a flick of my thumb nail
part of its shell slips off into the sheets.

Instead of feeling for it
I gaze in the hole
to see you come to bed again
burning hair with which
you carefully turn the mattress into flames
and through them
I can peer into a gloomy ward

or factory hall
on each side a row of beds
lead down endlessly
and I see at first
a thousand loins thrusting
as a thousand hips shuttle and sigh
but the sighs are from strangulation
and the lovers' hands are straining
at each others' throats,
while further down
the rest have given up all pretense of duty
wrestling and punching
the sacks of flesh beside them into bruises
until from sheer exhaustion
they lie in one another's arms
waiting in the half light
for the prod to come
and the struggle to begin again.

I would have gone in further
if you hadn't put your palm
upon the opening hole,
looking up for your eyes
as I caught them
a long fine hair
        was slowly drawn down
through the yolk
        between us
and I knew you knew
we could never be together
        unless the crisis turned.
You put the globe beneath
        the pillow
and we tried to sleep again.

[1975]

Today every inch

Today every inch
Of the city is in fever
The stillness of heat
At the breaking point
When your corpuscles
Carve their paths
Sometimes to life
Often to death.

What do you conclude
At six when you can still
Hear your breathing?
I want the dusk light
Roll its lips
Over my skin,
I have no other sphincter.

[1976]

It comes

It comes on
like my love
                    masturbates.
The windows swing
        in the rising wind
    against the walls
    of the welfare hotel,
    bottles on ledges
    fall
smashing
    their names.

Then a pause
rumbles, rumors
die far off

she stops and sighs
                as I float
        above the bed
        calling on the storm
    to return.

won't let this time
be idly spent
for she is not lazy
                in her pleasure,

the lightning
                tries again. . .
        and she moans
        while I count the shortest distance
                to orgasm,

Finally the rain,
    inevitable
  like the stone's weight,
    gulls cry
and when I asked her
    how she felt
  the rain
        responded.

[1976]

Dragonflies

"Ever seen dragonflies fuck?"
I said to him
on the first day of death.
"The dragonfly's tail
swings up
then comes down
to touch the other's
tail tip,
secreting such soft lumps
over the stream glint.

I chased them in Greece,
they were easier to catch
when they fucked,
with their purple-orange tails
twisting each into the other's,
then flung out to be sucked back,
their wing-nets trembling in the light.

A pleasure so simple
there is nothing inside it,
as simple as the pleasure
of crushing them
to get their powder
on my fingers."

No dragonflies here,
no hands even
to show you their flight
only a memory
of flashing tails
on the wet rocks,
giving color to the stream.
On the last day of death

let memory
return to the
dragonflies fucking.

[1977]

The Root of All Evil

Love weathers
Through the phone
all the powers
of touch and
motion gone
making the shaping
  of more than one kiss
impossible,
and even that
an accident
inside the
electricity
of mutual deception.

If I could name
what places me here
with all those craters
of states between NY and NH
I would make a placard
declaring:

The root of all evil
Is the lack of money,
Lack of credit cards,
Lack of telephone codes,
Lack of absenteeism,
Lack of quarter gas,
Lack of spare parts,
Lack of time to shape
        The act
            That would make
            The time,
Lack of terrified executives,
Lack of screams against them,

Lack of passion for such screams.
Lack of hope for such passion,
Lack of you, lack of the words and soul
To reach you. . .
The sin of these wages
Is that they're never enough.

[1977]

Self Portrait

Coffee bottom
Lemon rind and
Flecks of glass
Smashed
on the taverna floor,
Pissing in my pants
And dancing
Dancing with nothing
But coffee bottom
And now you say
I'm somber.

My prick is crooked
After so many erections
Squashed in my pants:
Rising from you
At the alarm
And stuffed down
To go to jobs
To unemployment halls
To this and that,
And so you say
I'm somber.

Never homeless,
At the bottom of every cup,
So bitter you will drink only
When you've forgotten me,
Distracted
And ready for the
Accidental.
So finally
You call me somber.

[1978]

The End of Zerowork

The dead remember everything,
Remember the blue box of addresses,
the tears on the stoop
the shadows of cups
after the final meeting.
They cry at our impotence,
Stretch their hands to us
"Oh! If we could only tell you."
They laugh
Shadowing our gestures
Humming over our talking,
Smiling at our naiveté
As we stumble into abysses
We don't even know we've fallen into.
They are sick of our defeats
Foretold
word for word
From each of their loved mouths
now so hated.

Words rise
from their graves
haunting us as we leave.
The dead lie with us
In our lonesome beds
As we rise in
the nightmare
of dawn.

[1978]

Urban Pioneer

"No more welfare tightrope for me,
I'm tired George,
don't make me feel guilty now.
Aren't you tired George?
So I'm urban pioneering,
Threw three house loads
Of black apaches out,
Renovated the houses,
And I'm about to collect the rent.

I paint the walls of the mental hospital white all
day,
I paint the cell walls clawed up from the night
before,
I even paint the faces of the patients white,
But you should see
How assertive I am now.
I walk into a store
With cash in my pocket
And don't cringe.

Why do I cringe with you?
I'm so tired.
So tired of you, so tired of me.
So tired I could swallow
The gallons of paint
I spread on my hands
In the morning."

[1978]

Coke can teach

Coke can teach you
private property
packed, protected,
even tighter than your ovaries
absolutely sacred
when folded in paper packets
of MINENESS

Was Karl Marx
snorting
beneath
the stars
in Lancaster?

I only wish
our nostrils
were wide enough

[1979]

I'm an old timer

I'm an old timer
and can't stand being embalmed.
Each time I glance to the left
I can trust
my friends to cremate me.
Let them breathe my smoke
and snort my ashes
to evoke memories
of our struggles
in their brains.

[1979]

My Art

My art is getting
expensive.
All it needed
once was a whiff
of lack of love
but now skin's
so rough
only the purest ice
piled in huge pieces
on a Maine beach
can turn the knife
down to blood.
At $100 a gram
I can't afford
much more than a haiku.

[1979]

Experience of Paradise

Bathing in the sink
In my uncle's orange grove
Watching the Taygetus Mountains
Warm water running through my body

[2024]

1980s–1990s
Tales of Empire

Two Poems

Two poems
in four months
in Boston,
filled with images
of clogged cement
and furious speed
recoiling from
the walls of Somerville.
Now, car ripped off,
broke
and followed by
the comrades' whispers
I finally turn south
to New York.
I'd rather be
mugged.

[1980s]

My hands are full

My hands are full
of honey and blood
stuck to the steering wheel.
The sun is glutting me with light
as the car floats down Highway 27.

[1980s]

Patras 1981

All your
Diseases are foretold
By the gypsy with
Heart troubles.

Bees mumble
And stutter your death
In the bluest of apiaries

And I'm
Going Down
To the Kalamata station
Drowned in green water,
As the light
Whirls into the whirling bottom

[1981]

Empire

In an obscure corner of the empire
With a dusty floor and malarial thoughts
The past comes to haunt me.

Memories
Of months before I left
Memories of poisoned cats.
On that August night
When I dug the hole to bury Daniel
And placed his limp grey body in the dark
I knew I dumped the dirt
On my years
In Brooklyn. . .

Now the Harmattan wind
Swirls through my window
Telling me it was Romano's son, Richie,
Who poisoned Daniel,
Poisoned Gatino
And poisoned my time.

He nervously came by, each week
To see if his mother and the ceiling
Had yet to fall,
Since Renaissance Realty said
In no uncertain terms
That to sell
He'd have to get rid of us all.

Who was Daniel, after all,
But the maladjusted,
tail-sucking pet
Of maladjusted symps
His crazy mother was soft on.

Bursting with impatience
for the dough,
Richie's stroke-prone brain
Set to work
What is poison?
What is suffocation?
What is death anyway?

Some days in the afternoon
I go to the smugglers' landing
On the Qua
To cool my fever
And hear
The river murmur.

[1984]

Going to Nigeria
(for John)

On a hot May night
you too tense to study the Law
and I too sick with Posthumous Notes,
we walked by Jamaica Pond,
firefly fragrant in the lamppost light,
trying to breathe a calm
off the black water.

As we walked
there slowly rose,
a dry stench of fear
fear of others
twisting every bend.

We are all now citizens in Murder.
Another spring is passed.
The burning smell
of Harmattan begins.
The fear lingers.

[1984]

Holiday Sloth

The metaphysical fallacy
of curtains
in the Harmattan wind
this Christmas day.
I, hungover,
and as lazy as dust
can only hear
murmurs saying
in the yard below:
"No misconduct,
No problems
Here in Calabar today."

Good, I can
lay here enjoying
my holiday sloth.

[1984]

Hypochondriac Visions

I'll die laughing
laying in a bare room
with white walls
while a good breeze
blows in from the sea,
worrying about the boil on my hand
while a snake lies coiled,
ready to strike
beneath my bed. . .

or

I'll die laughing
driving a car
stuffed with coke,
stuck in a traffic jam
on the Williamsburg Bridge
some cold windy afternoon. . .
the lost East River
glaucous beneath me
while trucks of oranges sway,
the chords sing and snap,
and we tumble. . .

[Calabar 1986]

Ode to an African Heideggerian

*What philosophy essentially can and must
be is this: a thinking that breaks the paths
and opens perspectives of the knowledge
that sets the norms and hierarchies of the
knowledge in which and by which a people
fulfills itself historically and culturally, the
knowledge that kindles and necessitates all
inquiries and thereby threats all values.*

—Martin Heidegger, Rector, University of
Freiberg (1935)

Opening Prayer

God, we pray to you
Because we are here tonight
Having some fun
And we hope your spirit
Will be with us.

Question and Answer

Philosophy in a technically-oriented society?
I don't know
But don't they say
These sciences questions are really philosophical
matters?
Einstein, Quantum, Relativity theory. . .
Does God play dice?
Be careful.
I'm mischievous.
I want no arrogant questions
If you think you know

You don't belong here.
Socrates, he was humble,
He knew he knew nothing.
You know nothing.
What class are you?
Third year?
You haven't started yet.
Frame your question.
You spend you time in Delta Park?
They're all the same
Delta, Moremi, girls quarters.
Families are broken there.
Like to experiment with this type of prostitution?
Make sure your grades are high.
You fall below 2.75
You are out.
Grow up.
I'll say it again
Pregnancy is not an airborne disease.
Remember. There are girls
From good families on this campus.
Who is 16 here?
Raise, raise you hands.
Think I don't understand?
I had a girlfriend too.
But I never let it distract me.
You follow me?
Know what I mean?
When I was young
In Amsterdam
The police stopped me
I said no
Found out later it was a police inspector.
So I tell you know
I want this department to grow.
You're not serious? Get Out.
When I was teaching in the Midwest,

In the corn fields,
They called me Mr. Precisely.
I heard students say
I got a C from Precisely.
Precisely gave me a B.
I know America well,
And American blacks too.
Rascals.
American blacks are rascals.
You want people to listen to you?
You listen first.
With philosophy you go everywhere.
Forget this nonsense:
Philosophy leads to witchcraft.
You don't have to apologize.
You're a high flier;
you can go to law school.
Heard of medical ethics?
Business too needs philosophers these days.
Yes, we need more programs,
But those we got are good
We got Logic,
Introductory and Symbolic. . .
If we had the teacher
We would have Advanced too.
Am I making sense?
There are problems I know.
I support the government
But I'm depressed with inequality.
If you're right for the job
You should have it.
Notice how everyone wants to be Yoruba?
Abiola is not a Yoruba,
He's from Bendel.
But he says he's Yoruba.
He thinks it will help him do something.
Africans are not individualistic

We take care of our people.
I don't know much
But I know in the north
They've got more tractors than taxis.
Am I making sense?
Are you with me?
You go to my village
There is no water.
And they milk the hell out of you.
I haven't paid my water rates
For two months.
Now I must go to my neighbor's compound.
In Rivers they say they're not Ibo
But you know they are.
Civil war or not
Ibos haven't changed.
You follow me?
You with me?
He talks about capitalism
And how we need socialism
—I'm coming—I'M coming
Perhaps, I don't know. . .
If socialism is so good.
Why not?
I'll jump on the bandwagon.
But why borrow?
Marx was no African.
Why not find an African way?
He says I'm a bourgeois.
But I teach philosophy for a living
I never said I was a philosopher.
The money. Thank god for the money.
And what is he doing anyway?
He doesn't live in Choba.
He lives in his university home
Then he talks against the bourgeoisie.
Am I making sense

Do you know what I mean?
You follow me, right?
Thanks, thanks, thanks again.

[1986]

"Ode to an African Heideggerian" recalls quite faithfully the speech given by the head of a philosophy department in a university in southeast Nigeria.

A Love Poem For Silvia

Through all this can you see
this is a love poem to Silvia?
The repetition of it
in the forest of this life
gone far beyond the middle
with the bushes for trees.

Is this a love poem to Silvia?
Nat King Cole
with the flowing violins of the '40s
in this our Lagos.

Notes and loneliness.
"I'm not alone in the night,"
An archaic hesitation
In a language long forgotten
From its roots
Do I speak to you?
"Love letters straight from your heart."

Mounds of dirt,
ditches, wrenched pipes,
dear Lagos
a collection of shards
without the slightest shame or recrimination
Christmas lights in June and all. . .

"Brazilian love bird
Fly to the one I love."
Never more did I know
My Silenus mask.
Night comes down once more,
The players appear again.

[Xmas 1986]

Afternoon naps

Afternoon naps
always end in
trying to remember
who I am,
my age and
the distance to my end,
among the sounds of life
and the full sun
in the window.
So it would feel
if I rose from the
dead.

[1986]

"Dry Souls are Best"
—Heraclitus

Harmattan smells
of a dusty office
where through
a broad unwashed window
blows a 2 o'clock light
on the Cube Steak Inc.'s books,
and on my father
erasing and adding
with a care I'll never know
while I wait for him
watching the dust motes.

Dust he was to me then
and his memory has vanished now.
He too has dried his soul
and floated into that silent volume
of illuminated dust.

I try to roll his life
as a nugget between my fingertips
assaying its weight and worth
only to feel my own dusty skin
in the Harmattan.

[Calabar 1986]

Adelabu "Square"

Adelabu "Square"
with Tripoli and Zaria on my mind,
Nothing like the fear of death
to make you repeat
the stupidest pleasures of life
As if repetition were
a sign of a useless,
longed for, indifferent immortality.

We play the same reggae tune,
try a new game of checkers and
drink the beer
over and over
pushing our luck
here on this square.

Dusk is nigh
once more and again
the globes of an ass
passes by, folded in cotton,
would that it would stop for me,
but no, it vanishes again.

Let's try another game of checkers.
The one that leers over the board
with the inquisitive eye
could have been a Lagos Zorba
if only I had been another Kazentzakis,
But we are neither,
except the players of the next game,
A new game
To give us the delight
of one more repetition.

[1980s]

On Hitting a Flying Roach with the Collected Works of T. S. Eliot

While lying in bed reading
I put my hand
in a forgotten coffee cup
on the floor,
my Calabar friend,
and you fluttered up
struggling through my fingers
flying away with your soft brown wings
to the wall near the ceiling,
your roachy whiskers
sighing for relief. . .

Our fortunes do change
in a blink.
A moment ago
you were breathing high
exquisite coffee dust
and sugared fumes,
but now
the whole volume
of T. S. Eliot's
Collected Works
Is flung in a stupid studied rage
Spinning for your head.
Can you forgive such knowledge?

[Spring 1984]

On International Travel

Left my friend that morning at the airport,
Heading for Nairobi
Where arrest and torture
May be waiting for him
In cells full of water and silence.

That evening
I boarded a Pan-Am flight for New York
Filled with U.S. Methodists
Coming from Kenya.
They were unanimous:
Kenyans were fine hosts
and the animals
were perfect specimens.

[Summer 1986]

Met my mother

Met my mother
on the road today,

    She didn't hug me,
    she didn't scold me,

but she smiled into my skin
    and went on her way.

[*October* 3, 1989]

Osiris Among the Dragonflies

Wives, Comrades, Enemies and Children
Scattered,
All scattered
As crumbs along the Nile.
And finally by the sea in Maine
Alone,
I hear the Taygetus stream
Still flowing
Down,

Through gleaming rocks
Dark pools and still,
Not knowing that they wait,
Are dragonflies,
Bluer than memory,
Hovering over the rush.

[1991]

George Caffentzis

War Poem

Rounding the bend
On the island road
Away from the ocean and its horizon
Back to the sight of oil, guns and money
In Portland Bay,
Hesitate to touch:
The harbor sludge,
The exploded, now decomposing bodies
And all the weight of the banks
To be broken each day
Just to breathe and work

"Pull back from this pain,
from the death of it,
pull back. . ."
the waters sing.

That is why I leave here,
No love can overcome this,
No love. . .
Coming out
of what
is common in us.

[Peaks Island — March 10, 1991]

53

Springtime in Maine

Everything is dripping
The gulls are ejaculating
And swirling
In a sun
That's just crossed the line.
The spring machine is here
And this poem
In protest must be penned.

[Peaks Island — March 26, 1991]

Pilgrimage to a transvestite saint

The bus for the holy transvestite's tomb
left late. By noon
it was hot
and time to stop
at the next taverna
on the side of the road.
There was lamb, tomatoes and bread
but you wouldn't touch it;
Your sister said, "Thanasi,
you're thin,
you'll die if you don't start eating. . .
here, eat this."
And you were thin,
thinner than many the Nazis worked to death.
She put the cut up meat in your plate.
You didn't open your mouth,
not even to say "No."

The sun's heat was cooled
by the cover of the taverna's trees,
but not your bloodshot eyes which were busy
burning pilgrims down
with the immolating images they emitted.
I only saw the fires then,
the images were mysteries
you wouldn't explain.
I only heard about them after you died:
they were the jangling heads of
decapitated communists
tied by their hair to your donkey's saddle
as you came down,
young and grim,
from the mountains.
Your eyes spit each of their teeth

like melon seeds to the ground,
burning the grass around us.
You could see no more
you could only spit.

The images came from '49.
But the brothers of the headless
Ones called you constantly
in the summer of '86.
Whenever I went to your house,
the phone was ringing and ringing;
the receiver trembled
and sometimes it leaped
off the hook.
You quickly put it back
but neither you nor anyone else dared to answer.

Your sister came back from the US
when she heard about the ringing
and thought the only way to stop it
was to go on a pilgrimage
to drink the miraculous water
springing at a transvestite saint's
execution spot.
Why? I couldn't understand then
but you might now.
Do you remember the story,
as convoluted as the roots
on the rock above her grave?

It's the story of the daughter
of an old and son-less father
during the Byzantine days
when every man had to send a son or go himself
to war.
It's the story of how she dressed as a man
and went to the army instead of her father.

Of her success in battle and quick promotion to
general.
Of the unrequited love of a prostitute,
who, trying to win her, claimed she had a child
from her.
Of the paternity trial
forcing the general to confront a monstrous
dilemma:
Prove s/he couldn't father the child or marry the
prostitute.
Of how she decided not to marry the prostitute,
defy the law and be executed
not to reveal her identity
since her father would be killed for breaking the
law.

After her death
she was stripped for burial and her secret was
revealed,
but for her faithfulness to the lies and cowardice
of her father
she was laid in honor in a stone tomb
and immediately on her corpse
a spring began to flow from the stone,
showing god's approval of her deed
and proving her sainthood.

The miracle waters from the tomb
were said to cure all the torments
of those who hid a deadly secret.

In the transvestite's valley later
that afternoon you stood silent
far away from the pilgrims who waded into the
stream
and drank the water.
Your sister brought you a Coke bottle full

and you wondered for a second
then, as a last hope,
you drank it and coughed.
As we got on the bus
to return to your house,
your sister was soothing you,
saying the calls would stop now.
And you could hardly believe it,
for your bile was thick enough to resist
huge doses of water magic.

On returning to the town,
the transvestite's spirit had died
and you didn't bother to return home,
for as we approached in the night
even the chickens were ringing.

[1993]

"We have sold all this to ourselves."
—J. M. Keynes

I am a shopkeeper to myself,
as I wander through the markets
I lure myself with a significant glance
to my wares
glittering precisely in my retina.
"Come," I say,
in alley after alley,
"I have something for you,
beautiful and cheap,"
and as I approach,
spread before me on carpets and tables,
all things are full of infinite attraction,
and I see myself buying,
selling myself through turns and twists
onto new vistas of desire

I never knew what was there.
Out they come,
the bills kept so darkly in my pocket,
as I delight in taking
them into my register.
Smiles meet smiles,
glances join eye beams
to new things. . .
new sales and more sales. . .
my satisfaction seems endless
until I'm all sold out.

[1993]

Dream

This is a dream of total loss. It is set in a Brooklyn feeling like the fifties, but it is not, because I see on 9th Street cars with long front ends, almost like expensive camera lens attachments, having difficulty turning corners.

I am at first with my mother walking on what feels to be Fifth Ave. Perhaps going on one of the interminable shopping expeditions she loved and I loathed.

Then I find myself alone walking west towards the Bay, excited to be exploring a new part of Brooklyn at first. As I approach the end of a street there is an arch and I can see the harbor in the distance. It is a beautiful climax.

But as I pass through the arch it suddenly feels like Rome or a Greek town. I am in an abandoned church square overrun with weeds and I stop. I first see what appears to be a mouse that turns into a rat moving in front of the door. As I follow it with my eyes it is transformed into a cat, a bit scruffy with a long nose. Relieved, I sit on a ledge and look over at what might be an abandoned well. There is a large dying insect, something like a mix of a scorpion and a roach, trapped in a web. The sun almost shines through it, though it is still twitching its members, trying to reach a smaller insect also in the web.

I move on. The feeling of Brooklyn in the spring on an early Sunday morning arises. All quiet, no one on the street, everything is normal, except me, walking alone. Suddenly I feel abandoned or having abandoned someone. . . it is my mother, where is she? Have I lost her? When did I lose her? How?

The shock is immobilizing. I stop, wondering where to go, and begin to cry.

[February 6, 1997]

Moon rhymes with June

After the meeting
where Lumumba's assassination was plotted,
the two junior Foreign Services officers
who took the minutes,
walked the shores of Lake Kivu
while "the biggest moon
in history rose"
to pull their blood together.

[2006]

2000s–
Memories and Encounters

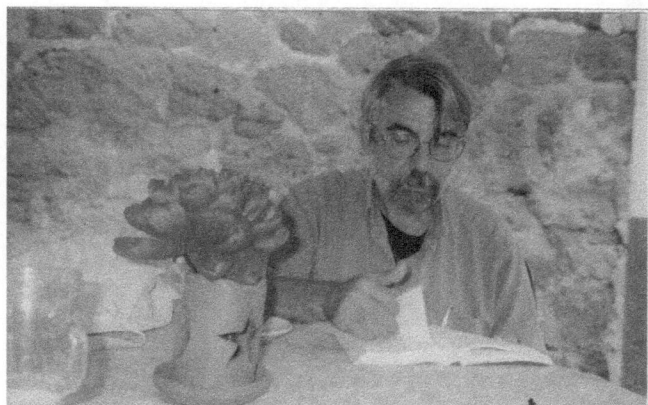

You never know

You never know,
    You never know,
what's come knocking at your door.

You never know,
    You never know,
who's walking across your floor.

Turn your hand,
    Turn over your hand,
to trace the lies of your life.

Your forgotten son,
    your misplaced daughter
come in the dark with a knife

to cut the rope from your wrists,
    to cut the gag from your mouth,
to ask,
    "Where have you been?"
    "Who has done this to you?"
and, worst of all,
    "What will you do now?"

[May 24, 2004]

The Swallows of Parma

My teachers,
the swallows of Parma,
swirl down
from the campanile to the piazza,
dawn to dusk,
their nervous bodies
starving for insects
invisibly latent in the air.

"O soul," they chirp to me,
"are you hungry,
with a hunger so abstract,
it kills you with frustration?
If so, do like us,
Sharpen your eyes and
Swirl,
      Swirl,
            Swirl.

[Parma — June 29, 2005]

Old Age

Old age was a new country once,
I entered it anxious,
as if by boat
slipping into its harbor
late in the night.
I gazed at the city lights,
wondering where I would find
a place to sleep.

I know its streets now
and in the afternoons
I pass the tenements
leaning precariously
on each other,
to sit in the once grand plazas of a fallen state,
the bushes overgrown
but fragrant in the spring,
dry and dusty in the late summer. . .
Counting the breathing of the sea
until I tire of it
and gaze down every boulevard
stretching to the horizon.

[March 27, 2006]

A Tale of Memory and Forgetting

I.
I thought memory was dust to me,
each move making a cloud
so I could hardly see
what was before me.

The dust will get so dense
one day,
there'll be no point in motion.
Nothing seen, smelled, tasted or touched
but more motes and moments of my old self.
Then it will be time to die.

I now watch the waves
off Mt. Desert Isle
through the spindrift
of ten thousand fragments
of memory.
Not just other seas,
but the black water
of the Niger Delta creeks,
and the cicadas
rasping in the heat
of the summer fields near Sparta.

Is there no small rain of oblivion,
no cloud burst of forgetting
to drench myself in?
A forgetting so strong
I'll not even remember this poem.
Will I ever be fresh again?

II.
And then,
just as I made the wish,
these faces rose
like steam whirls
from the dry earth
at the break of Harmattan
to question me.

My mother was first,
angry beyond words and action,
She wanted to know
why I,
want to forget her?

Other dead shimmer,
my father among them,
far in the distance of my flesh,
demanding an explanation.
Are they to be forever
erased from me?

Lovers smile from different directions,
confirmed again
in their estimation
that men like me
never stop being children,
especially as they become old.

But beyond them all
far back on the horizon
huge clouds are forming
from the smoke
of the students bodies' at Lubumbashi,
killed and burned,
from the cold fog
enveloping the bare toes of women

walking through the stone streets
of San Christobal at dawn,
from the gazes of eyes
on death row
heavy clouds,
accumulating pain, hatred and desire,

Roll down
dark with rain
to wash away
even this age.

[2006]

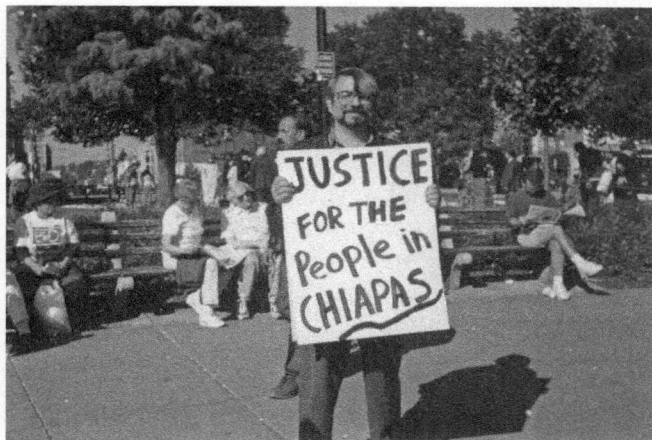

It or I

I stared through death
in my face
each morning
not seeing it,
since I looked
over my shoulder,
to catch it stalking me.
But death is no thief in the night.
It is reflected in every mirror,
Smiling or grimacing,

calling or receiving.
It is not an it,
  It is I.

[April 2007]

Isis in Parma
For Silvia

Walking the Parco Ducale this afternoon
Your mother's precise walk
Passed me by
In the legs and hips of another, taller woman
And in that instant
I became Isis
Stitching together
A thousand gestures torn from her
and scattered in a thousand bodies
To make the only eternity
That is still Dina.

[2009]

Poem for Sol Yurich

Thebes is nothing like you envisioned it, Sol.
I barely noticed it as the train passed it.
Thebes is now a small town in a plain of wheat
and grapes;
The IMFers of Tirisias' time and our own
Would think nothing of it
While you have grown wide in death
Reaching to the horizon and filling every molecule
In between.

Speak to me, Sol
About Thebes, Oedipus and the burning of the
Bank of America,
Speak to me. . .
So I can hear
the dry liberating bitterness of your voice
once more
Until you too step
Beyond the edge of things.

[June 1, 2013]

Poem for Joe Grange

Dear Joe,

You have become, for now, the background radiation
That remains since the origin of the universe,
as eternal as anything will ever be.
I hear your voice warming me
While drinking coffee,
While turning a corner,
While washing my face. . .
I can't let you go.

I've hesitated for months to write this poem.
For when it ends, with its final period,
I'll finally know
You are dead
and gone...

Love, George

[September 2014]

Buenaventura

Boy sleeping in the doorway
Of the Lemon Club,
One leg folded over the other,
The rain, the rain falls
Gently
As if to cup him
In its hand.
Where are we going
This morning?

[Buenaventura, Colombia — April 27, 2016]

AKA Death

I'm drooling in the day now,
It used to be only in the night.

I'm pissing in my pants now
While waiting for the train.

My tears are purely utilitarian now,
To clear out the crud accumulating 'round my eyes.

All these liquids liquidate me
inside and out. . .

AKA Death (Also Known As)

[New York — December 5, 2016]

Guatemala City at Easter-time [3]

Columns of names resurrected
After torture and death decades ago.
Long lists of names with nothing to clasp,
For lovers who've lost their loves,
Only a name to repeat night after night,
Night after night.

Are names enough
for justice?

[Guatemala City — March 15, 2018]

---

[3] When Silvia and I went to Guatemala City, we visited the main square and found remarkable columns. On each were the names of those murdered by the Ríos Montt regime in the 1980s. Their number was very high, in the thousands. 12,000 total, and yet a minuscule fraction of those who were massacred. The poem questions the power of these symbolic acts of remembrance given the lack of political accountability for Montt's killings.

Let boats sink

Silvia, Cara Mia,
Let bells ring
Boats sink
Cigars float
But never, never
Let me call off
arrows in flight.

Amo, Ama, Ami

[2023]

ABOUT THE AUTHOR

George Caffentzis, PhD, is an activist and Marxist scholar from Brooklyn, New York. His life has been devoted to analyzing and confronting the mechanisms of capital, from the anti-nuclear movement in the 1970s, student struggles in Nigeria in the 1980s, to the Zapatistas in Mexico in the 1990s, to the streets of Manhattan and the Occupy movement in the 2000s, and beyond. Caffentzis' work on the philosophy of money, the IMF and the World Bank, machines, work, and the ever-present energy crisis, was solidified as a founding member of the Midnight Notes Collective and continued in his books *In Letters of Blood and Fire: Work, Machines, and the Crisis of Capitalism* and *No Blood for Oil: Essays on Energy, Class Struggle and War*, among others. He is also the author of an academic trilogy on the philosophies of Locke, Berkeley, and Hume. *At the Edge of Everything* is his first published book of poems spanning his youth in New York and Greece, life in Nigeria, struggles and travels across the globe, to the present day.

ABOUT COMMON NOTIONS

Common Notions is a publishing house and programming platform that fosters new formulations of living autonomy. We aim to circulate timely reflections, clear critiques, and inspiring strategies that amplify movements for social justice.

Our publications trace a constellation of critical and visionary meditations on the organization of freedom. By any media necessary, we seek to nourish the imagination and generalize common notions about the creation of other worlds beyond state and capital. Inspired by various traditions of autonomism and liberation—in the US and internationally, historical and emerging from contemporary movements—our publications provide resources for a collective reading of struggles past, present, and to come.

Common Notions regularly collaborates with political collectives, militant authors, radical presses, and maverick designers around the world. Our political and aesthetic pursuits are dreamed and realized with Antumbra Designs.

www.commonnotions.org
info@commonnotions.org

COMMON
NOTIONS